NATIONAL PARK
FOUNDATION

Ms. Janet Sears
3857 Stone Pointe Way
Pleasanton, CA 94588-8361

D0470400

Aloft!

Written by: Douglas M. Heller

Edited by: Bobbi Valentine

Photography (Unless Otherwise Noted):

Douglas M. Heller & Bobbi Valentine

Design & Production: Bette Brodsky

Registrations and Trademarks:

Albuquerque International Balloon Fiesta ®

Balloon Fiesta ®

Special Shape Rodeo ™

Special Shape Glowdeo™

Night Magic Glow™

Twilight Twinkle Glow™

America's Challenge™

AfterGlow™

Copyright 2011

Aloft Publishing LLC

www.aloftbooks.com

All rights reserved. All rights are reserved to the publisher. No part of this publication may be reproduced or transmitted in any form or by any means, electronic or mechanical, including photography, recording or any information storage and retrieval system, nor may the pages be applied to any materials, cut, trimmed or sized to alter the existing trim sizes, matted or framed with the intent to create other products for sale or resale or profit in any manner whatsoever, without prior permission in writing from the publisher.

ISBN: 978-0-615-43860-3

Printed in China

Aloft!
at the Albuquerque International Balloon Fiesta®

A welcome message from Governor Susana Martinez

As the Governor of New Mexico, it is my pleasure to congratulate the Albuquerque International Balloon Fiesta on its 40th year. Thanks to the annual fiesta, hot air balloons have become an iconic symbol of our state and a world renowned event that attracts visitors from around the world. Since the sport of ballooning transcends all languages and nationalities, it is an honor for the Land of Enchantment to host this grand international event.

As we reach this milestone, it is a privilege to welcome back the hundreds of pilots who participate each year in the Albuquerque International Balloon Fiesta and to celebrate the past 39 years. We are confident that this years' special 40th celebration will be filled with great energy and enthusiasm.

A special thanks also goes out to the *Aloft!* publishers, for its visual expression of the balloon fiesta. Your publication captures the history and spirit of the event.

While in New Mexico, I hope that you discover the great treasures the Land of Enchantment has to offer—like our rich history and friendly people. Also, make sure you take time to experience our state's majestic sunsets and sample our renowned cuisine and visit our art galleries and museums which showcse the diversity of our state. Enjoy your experience at the 40th Albuquerque International Balloon Fiesta and in the Land of Enchantment.

Bienvenidos a Nuevo Mexico!

Sincerely,

S Martinez

Susana Martinez
Governor of New Mexico

Aloft! is dedicated to the memory of
Richard Abruzzo and Carol Rymer Davis

B oth avid balloonists and long time participants in the
Albuquerque International Balloon Fiesta, Abruzzo
(Albuquerque) and Davis (Colorado) won the 48th
Gordon Bennett Cup in 2004. Doing what they loved to do,
the two pilots perished in rough weather over the Adriatic Sea
while competing in the 2010 Coupe Aeronautique Gordon
Bennett Gas Balloon Race in Europe.

Contents

Introduction

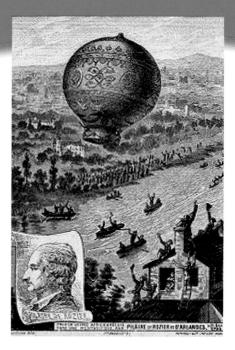

Modern day hot air ballooning did not become a reality until the late 1950's. It was the advent of the propane tank which provided an effective method of filling and sustaining the balloon (the envelope) with warm air. However, man's dream of flying among the birds had long been alive for over 200 years. In celebrating the 40th Albuquerque International Balloon Fiesta, we take a brief look back at how the dream was born, and highlight some ballooning milestones that left their mark in history.

The first attempt at untethered manned balloon flight actually began with a sheep, duck and rooster. Two French brothers, Joseph-Michel and Jacques-Etienne Montgolfier both scientists and inventors had been working in their father's paper manufacturing business, located in the

south of France. One day while burning some paper, they noticed ashes floating in the air above the chimney. They decided to test this theory and held burning paper under the opening of a bag, called a "balon" made from paper and linen, slowly as the bag filled with warm air it floated upward.

After many months of successful experimentation, the Montgolfier brothers went to Paris to construct their largest balloon yet, made from paper and cloth. They had determined that the combined use of straw, dried horse manure and wool would best serve as their fuel source; experience found these items would generate smoke without much flame, which reduced the risk of catching the balloon on fire. At the time the brothers believed that it was the smoke, not the heat that had the special power of lift. On the 19th of September 19, 1783 at the Palace of Versailles, the Montgolfier brothers successfully completed the launch of their balloon, which stayed aloft for eight minutes before landing safely in a field. Far too nervous to fly themselves, they had placed a sheep, a duck and rooster aboard a suspended basket. This monumental flight took place in front of Louis XVI, Marie Antoinette, the French court and a crowd of more than 100,000 people.

On the heels of their success, the Montgolfier brothers wanted to seal their invention, so they approached the King of France and requested that they be allowed to fly a second balloon with humans aboard rather than farm animals, and he agreed. Wasting little time, only two months following the ascension at Versailles, Joseph-Michel and Jacques-Etienne made history with the first manned untethered free flight of a hot air balloon on November 21. Standing on a round platform suspended below the balloon as it went aloft were scientists and close friends of the brothers, Pilatre de Rozier and Francois Laurent le Vieux d'Arlandes. They ascended about 500 feet in the air floating over the roof tops of Paris before safely landing in a field several miles from where they had launched.

History was made that day . . . however, it was just the beginning!

In 1785, two years following the first manned flight, a French balloonist, Jean Pierre Blanchard, and his American copilot, John Jefferies, became the first to cross the English Channel in a balloon. At the time, the English Channel was considered one of the challenges of long distance ballooning.

Later that same year, Jean Pilatre de Rozier, became the first person in history not only to fly but also to die in an air accident when his hybrid balloon encompassing two envelopes, one filled with hydrogen and the other hot air, exploded while trying to cross the English Channel.

January 7, 1793 marked another milestone when the French pilot Blanchard became the first to fly a balloon in North America . . . George Washington was present for his ascension.

In August of 1932, a Swiss balloonist and scientist Auguste Piccard achieved an altitude record of 52,498 feet, the first human to reach the stratosphere. Altitude rather than distance became the newest challenge for balloonists to beat.

In 1935, "Explorer 2", the experimental helium-filled balloon with a pressurized suspended capsule, set a new altitude record of 72,395 feet and held that benchmark for the next 20 years. This ballooning milestone paved the way for aviation and future space travel, proving that a human could sustain themselves in a pressurized chamber at extreme altitudes.

In 1960, Captain Joe Kittinger broke two records, one for altitude when his balloon reached an elevation of 102,000 feet, and the second for the highest altitude parachute jump. Kittinger's rate of descent was so fast, that his body broke the sound barrier as he re-entered earth's atmosphere.

In 1978, Ben Abruzzo, Maxie Anderson and Larry Newman piloting the "Double Eagle II", became the first balloonists to cross the Atlantic Ocean. After many failed attempts by members of this team and several other teams trying to make this crossing, the three achieved success in their specially constructed helium-filled balloon. In the process they set a new aloft time record.

In 1981, the gas-filled "Double Eagle V" successfully completed the first Pacific Ocean crossing. The team of Ben Abruzzo, Larry Newman, Ron Clark and Rocky Aoki set a new distance record of 5,768 miles, launching from Japan and landing in Mendocino, California 84 hours later.

In 1987, the first Atlantic crossing in a hot air balloon (rather than helium-filled) was successfully completed by Richard Branson (Founder of Virgin Group) and Per Lindstrand (Swedish aeronautical engineer and founder of Lindstrand Balloons). The team completed their 2,900 mile journey in a record-breaking time of 33 hours, flying with an envelope capacity of 2.3 million cubic feet, the largest balloon ever flown at the time.

In 1991, Branson and Lindstrand teamed up again becoming the first hot air balloonists to cross the Pacific Ocean. Launching from Japan and landing in Canada, the pair set a new long distance record, traveling across 6,700 miles in 47 hours and reaching speeds of more than 240 mph.

In 1999, pilots Bertrand Piccard and Brian Jones successfully completed the first around the world balloon flight in a specially constructed "Rozier" balloon (named for its inventor), lifted by separate compartments of helium and hot air. Launching from Switzerland, the pair obliterated all previous long distance records staying aloft for almost 20 days before finally landing in Africa.

Now having enjoyed a brief history of ballooning, please come share the excitement and joy of *ALOFT! at the Albuquerque International Balloon Fiesta . . .* the greatest ballooning event on the planet!

Balloon Fiesta Overview

BALLOON FIESTA . . . AND ITS HUMBLE BEGINNINGS!

The Albuquerque International Balloon Fiesta has been touted as the largest event of its kind in the world. If you have been one of those lucky enough to attend, then you might agree, seeing 500 or more hot air balloons aloft above the Rio Grande Valley leaves one awestruck.

Ballooning in Albuquerque has a long history which can be traced as far back as 1882. It was then when "Professor" Park Van Tassel, owner of the Elite Saloon, purchased an early form of a balloon for $850, considered a large amount of money for the time. He planned on launching his balloon as part of a 4th of July celebration. He began inflating the envelope late afternoon of the proceeding day with coal gas. This mixture consisted of hydrogen, methane and carbon dioxide, a concoction made

The first balloon rally in Albuquerque, at the Coronado Mall in 1972.

by burning coal in a low-oxygen environment. Considered Albuquerque's first ascension, Van Tassel finally launched his balloon to a gathering crowd late afternoon on the 4th, with his envelope only two thirds full. He made plans to fly again that year during the second annual New Mexico Territorial Fair held in September. However, in the process of moving the inflated balloon to the fairgrounds, it was accidentally released by the crew and ended up exploding after reaching an altitude of approximately 5,000 feet.

Numerous flying attempts continued to take place in and around Albuquerque over the next seventy-five years. Piloting balloons in the early days was clearly an act of trial and error and in many cases it was more error than trial. Some envelopes exploded while other balloons and baskets plummeted to the ground. There was also a noted case of a pilot's parachute getting blown open ushering him out of the basket and into the air.

Early methods of inflation were a mixed bag of experimentation, ultimately trying to achieve the appropriate quantity and mixture of gases required in order to get the balloon, pilot and any passengers off the ground and in the air. Coal gas inflation previously mentioned, seemed to be the method of choice in the beginning, possibly because few other reliable alternatives existed at the time. Other forms of hydrogen also came into use, sometimes in combination with coal gas, but early on the fuel was concocted from iron fillings and sulfuric acid, and not always the safest. It was not until the late 1950's when a U.S. government research program built a hot air balloon and inflated it with air heated by a propane flame...from which the "modern" hot air balloon was born.

Balloon Fiesta itself had very humble beginnings. Some forty years ago back in the summer of 1971, a gentleman by the name of Sid Cutter, of Cutter Aviation fame (formerly known as Cutter Flying Service), wanted to do something very special and unique for his mother's birthday. He decided to purchase a hot air balloon to be inflated and tethered as the centerpiece of her celebration. The following day, Sid and his brother Bill ended up taking an unscheduled flight, when their crew accidentally released the tied rope letting the balloon go aloft in the skies above Albuquerque. Both Sid and Bill were experienced fixed-wing pilots, though neither had previous balloon piloting experience at the time. However, once back safely on the ground, Sid's ballooning vision was born. In the fall of that year, Cutter and eight other friends founded the local balloon club, known as the Albuquerque Aerostat Ascension Association, which they nick-named the "AAAA" or "Quad A". The club purchased a balloon; they named "Roadrunner" and signed up members who wanted to learn to fly. Roadrunner made its maiden flight in early January 1972.

That same year, KOB Radio of Albuquerque was planning their 50th Anniversary and wanted to celebrate with an unusual event. Sid Cutter at the time was interested in organizing the first hot air balloon rally in New Mexico, and KOB decided that they would sponsor the rally for their anniversary. Previously, the largest recorded gathering of balloons was a total of 19 assembled for a rally in England. KOB and the New Mexico rally organizers were determined to beat that record by holding the biggest balloon rally ever. Cutter and the "Quad A" Club were successful in signing up 21 balloonists from Arizona, California, Colorado, Iowa, Michigan, Minnesota, Nevada and Texas. It was, however, unfortunate that many registered pilots did not arrive in time for the scheduled event. So on a chilly Saturday morning in April, 13 balloons inflated on the dirt parking lot west of the Coronado Shopping Center. Tom Rutherford, an exuberant announcer from KOB had stirred up much excitement over this scheduled balloon rally. This resulted in over 10,000 people showing up to watch the multi-colored hot air balloons launch and drift away from the shopping center.

As fate would have it, Don Kersten, an official of the Balloon Federation of America was among the crowd that day. The Federation Aeronautique Internationale[1] had directed Kersten to select a site for the first world hot air ballooning championship. He was so impressed with Albuquerque after seeing the rally, that he encouraged the city to submit a bid to host the world championship. Cutter and Rutherford organized World Balloon Championships Inc. and submitted the only bid to be the host city. They later learned that Kersten had approached no city other than Albuquerque. In February 1973, Albuquerque

Sid Cutter, one of the most imprtant early figures in Albuquerque ballooning history.

hosted its second Balloon Fiesta in concert with the first World Hot Air Balloon Championship. The event was held at the State Fairgrounds, with 138 balloons registered from 13 countries.

1. The FAI is a non-governmental and nonprofit international organization which encourages and oversees the conduct of sporting aviation events throughout the world and certifies aviation world records. The FAI was founded by representatives from Belgium, France, Germany, Great Britain, Italy, Spain, Switzerland, and the United States, meeting in Paris on Oct. 14, 1905. In 1999 the FAI headquarters moved from Paris to Lausanne, Switzerland.

BALLOONS BY THE NUMBERS

How did a small gathering of 13 balloons in 1972 grow into Albuquerque becoming the hot air ballooning capital of the world? There are several factors contributing to its success. One is the weather of the Rio Grande Valley and second, is the unusual occurrence of the "box" effect. Combine this with the fortunate timing of Albuquerque hosting the first World Hot Air Balloon Championship in 1973, consisting of 138 balloonists from 13 countries, and from that point on it became the place the pilots wanted to fly.

Just five years later in 1978, the number of registered balloons at Balloon Fiesta had doubled to 278. In 1988, registration had grown to 600, including 10 special shapes and 10 gas balloons. Gas balloons saw their first registration in 1981, and now play a major role at Balloon Fiesta with participation in the annual America's Challenge™ Gas Balloon Race.

In 1998, the third year in which Balloon Fiesta Park hosted the event, a total of 873 balloons had been registered. However, that number paled in comparison to the Balloon Fiesta held in 2000 where registration grew to a record level of 1,019 balloons. That year set a Guinness World Record for launching the most balloons in a given period of time. Subsequently, AIBF organizers realizing the strategic and physical limitations of both Balloon Fiesta Park and landing sites, decided to limit registration the following year to a maximum of 750 balloons. That number was trimmed once

more in 2009 to a limit of 600 registrations. The organizers felt this was a necessary step not only because of the continued growth of the Rio Grande Valley, but also because of greater limitations for landing sites.

The year 2008 was not a record-setting year for the Balloon Fiesta, but it had a strong showing in overall participation. A total of 621 hot air balloons had been registered, including 84 special shapes. In addition, 17 gas balloons participated, five teams in the America's Challenge Gas Race and 12 teams contending in the Coupe Aeronautique Gordon Bennett Gas Race. Of these teams, 9 made a decision to fly using hydrogen as their fuel source while 8 flew with helium gas.

Registration for 2008 included 42 of the 50 states, as well as 22 other countries. International participants included: Belgium, Canada, Croatia, Czech Republic, Finland, France, Germany, Italy, Japan, Latvia, Lithuania, New Zealand, Panama, Poland, Russia, Scotland, Slovenia, South Africa, Spain, Switzerland, Ukraine and United Kingdom. Balloonists from many of these countries participate at the Albuquerque International Balloon Fiesta year after year knowing that its one of the premier places to fly in the world.

ATTENDANCE BY THE NUMBERS

People have always had a fascination for flying machines as far back as 1783. It was then that the Montgolfier brothers successfully launched farm animals in a balloon as man's first attempt at flight. This monumental event took place in at the Palace of Versailles in front of more than 100,000 spectators. Albuquerque's first Balloon Fiesta in 1972 didn't quite garner the same numbers with only approximately 10,000 people in attendance at the Coronado Shopping Center that day. At that point manned flight was no longer a novelty; however, people still seemed to be both fascinated and excited by the sight of colorful balloons going aloft in the skies above Albuquerque.

Since 1972 attendance at Balloon Fiesta has blossomed right along with the number of balloon registrations. Attendance levels tend to average in the 730,000 range over the nine day event. However, the 2007 Balloon Fiesta had broken all previous levels with approximately 899,466 people in attendance. That attendance record still stands today.

The Albuquerque International Balloon Fiesta has been touted as "the most photographed event in the world". Considering the average daily attendance is in the range of 80,000, one could hardly argue with this fact. Does it feel a little crowded on the launch field at times? Maybe, but everyone is too busy looking at all the magnificent balloons inflating and launching as part of the morning mass ascension to notice the other 79,999 people around them.

18

VOLUNTEERS BY THE NUMBERS

Let's take a moment to talk about the volunteers, because putting on the largest ballooning event in the world doesn't happen overnight or with a simple snap of the fingers. The planning for each year begins well before the preceding year's event is even over. A team of 16 full-time professionals handles the overall management of the Balloon Fiesta event. Their areas of responsibility include: Event Production which oversees all ballooning events, social events and pilot registration; Merchandising under which posters, official merchandise, and collectibles such as pins fall; Marketing, including advertising, corporate sponsorship, ticketing and membership programs; Field Maintenance of all Balloon Fiesta buildings and grounds during the event; Communications, including publicity and media relations; and Administration which manages human resources, finances and legal.

There are more than 1,000 dedicated volunteers working under this management team that gets involved each year to help make the Balloon Fiesta the great success it is. When attending the event everything appears to run pretty much like clockwork, but behind the scenes it involves a massive coordination effort. Volunteers do everything from taking event registrations; scheduling and controlling the large numbers of RV arrivals and departures, including the layout of their parking areas; they manage and direct traffic, including collecting parking fees and entry fees as well provide parking lot control . . . with 80,000 or more daily visitors this is no easy task; 2,000 additional volunteers also participate as chase crews for the pilots . . . helping launch and breaking down upon landing; volunteers manage all the official merchandise tents; provide crowd control during special balloon events; act as courtesy shuttle and cart drivers; provide staff services at VIP tents; and provide many other event tasks too numerous to mention.

Why is it important to highlight the volunteers? Attending this event now for several years and getting a chance to meet some of these people, leaves a lasting impression on you. Many of the same people return to participate every year; some have been volunteering for 30 or more years. Volunteers come from all walks of life and include staff from many area businesses, and members of local church groups. It's definitely an addictive sport, not only for those volunteering, but for the pilots and spectators as well, returning year after year.

BALLOON FIESTA PARK

The Albuquerque International Balloon Fiesta is the premier ballooning event in the world. It has gained this success due to its geographic location, its launch venue and open space (availability of landing sites). The launch field at Balloon Fiesta Park is capable of accommodating over 200 balloons in a single wave; the Rio Grande Valley provides the ideal flying conditions (especially in October); and the urban setting of the city easily handles the needs and services of the large number of spectators who attend each year.

Albuquerque's first organized Balloon Fiesta was held in 1972 on the grounds of the Coronado Shopping Center, located on the eastside of town. In 1975 the event was moved to Simms Field; it moved again in 1981 to Cutter Field, and then made its third move to what is known as Old Balloon Fiesta Park (landfill site) in 1985. Finally, in 1996 Balloon Fiesta landed at its current 360 acre park location on the northern edge of the city. The venue lies west of Interstate 25, bordered between Paseo Del Norte on the south and Roy Road on the north. Operated by Albuquerque's park system, with just over 100 acres currently developed, it is the city's largest park boasting not only Balloon Fiesta's launch field but also multiple sports fields, a driving range and the Anderson-Abruzzo Albuquerque International Balloon Museum.

The 72 acre launch field at Balloon Fiesta Park is equal in size to just over 56 football fields, with 208 official launch sites, accomodating a maximum of 415 balloons. Originally dirt, the field was seeded with grass beginning in 2000 using recycled water for irrigation. The grass-covered launch field helped to eliminate dust caused by the continuous movement of chase vehicle traffic entering and exiting the park. Even more importantly, it allowed balloon envelopes prepping for launch to be laid-out on a clean soil-free surface. Balloon envelopes typically are not washed or cleaned primarily because of the impact to the coating on the fabric. Furthermore, if not fully dried, mildew can form causing damage to the fabric and seams. Balloon crews generally keep large tarpaulins on-hand, that can be spread out and used to protect the envelope from either moisture when launching, and/or debris when packing up.

BALLOON FIESTA MILESTONES

There have been many memorable moments over the four decades of the Albuquerque International Balloon Fiesta, below are some of the highlights.

1973 First World Hot Air Balloon Championship

1989 First special shape event held with 35 balloons participating

1992 Kodak becomes title sponsor of the event (1992-2001)

1993 AIBF hosts the Gordon Bennett Cup Gas Balloon Race for the first time with the winning Austrian team of Josef Starkbuam and Rainer Roehsler flying 1,137.89 miles

1994 AIBF hosts the World Gas Balloon Championship

1995 First America's Challenge Gas Balloon Race held and has been part of Balloon Fiesta every year since

1996 AIBF holds event for the first time at Balloon Fiesta Park with 108 special shape balloons participating in the Special Shape Rodeo (largest ever)

2000 1,019 balloons participate in Balloon Fiesta, set a Guinness World Record for launching the most balloons in a set period of time

2005 Gas balloon pilots Bob Berben and Benoit Simeons of Belgium, participating in the Gordon Bennett Cup, travel 2,112 miles from Albuquerque to southeastern Quebec Province in Canada, setting the new record for farthest distance traveled. They were able to break the old record by 751 miles)

2007 AIBF estimated to have the largest attendance on record that year of 899,466 visitors

Mass Ascension

EARLY MORNING ARRIVAL

If you suffer from insomnia or regularly awake at 4:30 am or earlier (AKA "the ugly hour"), then Balloon Fiesta is just for you! However, if you're like most people, waking up, getting dressed and over to Balloon Fiesta Park can be a major ordeal . . . especially when trying to do this multiple days in a row. You're thinking to yourself while sipping coffee and getting dressed; "I don't fish, and if I did, I wouldn't go this early . . . must be nuts; am I going to be the only one at the park?"

Your fear is somewhat diminished when you turn on the TV at 5:00 am (the time the local networks start broadcasting from the park), and you can't believe your eyes seeing a few thousand spectators walking around on the launch field. But wait, you're now thinking OMG, I'm going to be late!

By the time you reach the roadway into Balloon Fiesta Park, at around 5:30 am, (mind you it's still pitch dark out), there is a line of tail lights as far as the eye can see. Now sitting in bumper to bumper traffic as you inch your way into the parking lots, you're kicking yourself saying . . . why didn't I get here earlier? Don't worry; the other 79,999 people attending Balloon Fiesta that day are probably thinking the same thing. However, there are some fortunate ones, like the RV goers who are able to avoid the early morning traffic, by reserving one of the several thousand designated parking spaces in lots next to Balloon Fiesta Park.

There is a good reason for this "ugly hour" madness, which, by the way, is much more acceptable when the weather is mild and you're not standing around freezing your tail off, and that's to watch the illuminated launch of "Dawn Patrol" between 5:45 and 6:00 am. Now if you need sustenance to keep yourself going until mass ascension, which occurs around 7:00 am, head for the food concessions, where you can feast on a funnel cake or chow down a breakfast burrito, yum!

CHASE CREWS

Whether launching a single balloon or 500 as part of mass ascension, they all require the assistance of chase crews. Many pilots coming to an event such as Balloon Fiesta will drive and trailer their equipment, bringing along family or friends as the crew. However, for some pilots this isn't possible, especially for those traveling a great distance or coming from overseas where the envelope and gondola are shipped to the destination. In these cases, volunteer chase crews and sometimes chase vehicles are provided locally. The challenge, at an event such as Balloon Fiesta is finding enough people who are available to work nine consecutive days. The number of the crew required for each balloon will depend on the size of the envelope and the gondola, as the bigger you go, the more man-power you need for launch preparation and break-down upon landing. On an average 4-5 crew are required to prep a balloon for launch and retrieve and pack it up upon landing.

ground. This could include setting down within restricted zones, private properties, behind fences or gates, in the middle of fields or on public roadways. If all the stars are aligned the chase vehicle will have drive-up access to the landing site. Otherwise, hauling out the equipment is not anyone's idea of a good time with typical envelopes weighing several hundred pounds and gondolas even more.

Volunteering as part of a chase crew can be great fun, providing a close up and personal experience of ballooning. One must keep in mind however, that crewing does involve a little work along the way. Launch preparation includes off-loading the gondola, envelope, burner system, and inflate fans, along with other bits and pieces from the chase vehicle. It's then a matter of setting up the gondola and getting the envelope ready for inflation. The chase begins once the pilot has successfully launched, (hopefully without the vehicle keys in their pocket). Communications are maintained via a two-way radio system, typically initiated by the pilot. Tracking the balloon can be exhilarating as long as the individual driving obeys all the traffic laws and does not get distracted by what's up in the air, which should be the job of a fellow crew member. Sometimes the challenge for chase crews is getting to the landing site. Balloons have little navigational control; therefore, pilots are never quite sure where they'll ultimately land until on the

Chase vehicles come in all shapes and sizes from your basic pick-up truck to small RV's with trailers. Some pilots like to travel in style arriving in SUV Mercedes with a custom trailer attached, while others go the classic route, hauling their ballooning equipment in vintage pick-up trucks. Then there is the pilot who likes to be unique, using an old fire truck as the chase vehicle. Basically, it's "anything goes" for getting pilot, crew and equipment from point A to point B.

THE COLD & HOT AIR INFLATION

The Albuquerque International Balloon Fiesta encompasses such a large number of balloonists that each is assigned one of 208 grid locations on the launch field, which are denoted by short white pylons displaying a number. Each grid location can accomodate 1 or 2 balloons, depending on their size. The assigned grid location for each balloonist will remain the same throughout the nine day event. Upon arrival at the launch site, the pilot and crew will begin the setup process. This entails removing the gondola (also referred to as the basket), envelope, burner system, superstructure frame, and inflation fan(s) from the chase vehicle. Typically, a four passenger balloon will require the assistance of 4-5 crew members.

32

While the pilot attaches the support frame, burner system and propane tank(s) to the gondola, the crew works on preparing the envelope for inflation. Having first removed the envelope from its storage bag, it is then spread out in its flattened shape on the ground. Once the gondola has been fully assembled, the pilot will conduct several test fires of the burner system to ensure that all components are working properly. The outfitted gondola is now ready to be placed on its side at the bottom or "mouth" of the envelope. The envelope and gondola are then connected to one another with rigging lines, which are attached at the top of the superstructure frame.

Before the envelope can be filled with warm air, it must first become inflated with ambient air, this is known as "cold air inflation". One to two gas-operated fans (depending on the size of the envelope) are placed on either side of the gondola directing air flow towards the mouth of the envelope. Two to four crew members and/or passengers assist by holding open the mouth of the balloon to allow the fan-driven air to fill the envelope.

As the envelope inflates, the crew will check the "crown" of the balloon (the opening at the top of the envelope). This is to make sure that Velcro tabs which fix a large flap of fabric over the opening is secure. This opening is also referred to as a "parachute valve". The deflation line for this valve runs down inside the envelope to the gondola allowing the pilot to "dump" or release hot air to either slow the balloon's ascent, or control its descent. Opening this valve upon landing provides rapid deflation, preventing the envelope from dragging the gondola. The crown of the balloon also contains a sturdy handling line called the "crown line". As the envelope starts to fill with air, one or two crew members, wearing leather gloves, will walk the line straight back from the crown of the balloon keeping it taut in the process. This is required in order to keep the envelope steady downwind and minimize any side to side rolling motion. Once the balloon is righted the line will be walked back and secured to the gondola.

With the cold air inflation nearly complete, the pilot will enter the envelope for a pre-flight inspection of the fabric, rigging lines and parachute valve. Once the envelope is "fat" with ambient air, the gas fans are turned off, and the pilot steps into the gon-dola to ignite the propane burner(s) heat-ing up the inside air. This action will cause the balloon to rise, up-righting the gondola. Simultaneously, several crew members will be holding down its sides to ensure that the balloon does not launch prematurely before any passengers climb on board. The pilot will continue to fire the burners which results in short blasts of hot air displacing the cold air allowing the balloon to become "light" and ready for launching.

THE "BOX" EFFECT

April originally served the date of Balloon Fiesta, as the chilly spring mornings were well suited for flying. Eventually, however, the event was moved to early October where the combination of cooler weather and more favorable wind patterns provided the "ideal" flying conditions known as the "Albuquerque Box".

The Box can be found in many valleys, but nowhere is it more common then in Albuquerque. The Rio Grande Valley appropriately situated at the base of the Sandia Mountains

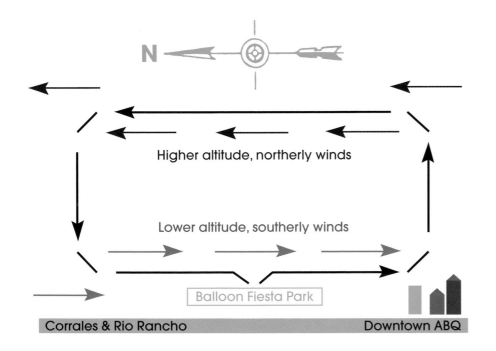

provides for a temperature inversion condition allowing dense stable cool air to form in the river valley, resulting in the Albuquerque Box. During nighttime hours, the air within a few hundred feet of the ground is cooled by radiant conditions. This low level inversion is more likely to occur when clear skies, low humidity, and light winds exist. This cool air, like water flows to the lower elevations. In Albuquerque, this air will flow down the river valley to the south. When the upper prevailing winds flow toward the north, you have the Box. As the sun rises over the Sandia Mountains heating the ground, the lower, cooler air is also heated and mixes with the higher layers of air thereby dissipating the Box effect generally by mid-morning.

The Box effect is more likely to take place in late summer through October, occurring on average 30% of the time. When present, it creates a series of predictable wind patterns, which allow pilots the ability to navigate direction depending on the balloon's altitude. At lower altitudes the winds tend to be southerly, but at higher elevations they tend to be directed north. During a mass ascension, one can observe a grouping of balloons at a given altitude flying in one direction, while at a different altitude, their movement will be seen in the opposite direction. Pilots utilize these changing winds to navigate in a vertical box: they ascend slightly from the launch field moving south, ascend higher and move north; descend, and repeat the Box or land back on or near Balloon Fiesta Park.

DAWN PATROL

One of the main reasons that Fiesta goers start arriving at Balloon Fiesta Park at the ungodly hour of 5:00 am is to watch the Dawn Patrol rise from the launch field into the darkened skies of the Rio Grande Valley. The purpose of these early morning flights is to assess wind conditions and direction at various altitudes, and determine if the Box is in effect. Normally, Dawn Patrol will consist of up to ten or so balloons. Watching them launch in a lit choreographed fashion in the early morning hours can be an awe-inspiring sight.

The excitement builds from the moment the burners are test-ignited atop each gondola, appearing and sounding like fire-breathing dragons in the night. As they launch into the darkened sky, each balloon glows in a timed fashion from the heated air filling their envelopes, a beautiful and memorable sight it is!

Dawn Patrol goes aloft every morning of Balloon Fiesta, unless of course there are excessive winds or inclement weather conditions. The wind data they gather provides vital information to the balloonists participating in either mass ascension or special events occurring on the launch field that day. Ideally pilots like to see prevailing winds at no more than 10 mph. Beyond this level, landings can become more difficult. If conditions appear questionable, prior to launching pilots will release a helium-filled balloon into the air in order to evaluate wind speed and direction.

Dawn Patrol will typically begin their equipment preparation and cold air inflation just after 5:30 am, taking off around 6:00 am, approximately one hour before sunrise. Because these balloonists are flying in the dark their gondolas must include FAA approved lighting systems, in order to avoid not only each other while in flight, but other aircraft as well. Dawn Patrol began at Balloon Fiesta in 1978 after two California balloonists had developed lighting "position" systems, which allowed pilots to fly in the predawn hours. As pilots must be able to see the ground in order to determine a suitable landing site, those participating in Dawn Patrol stay aloft for 1 to 1½ hours from sunrise.

THE ZEBRAS

Much of the continued success of the Albuquerque International Balloon Fiesta can be attributed to the long running safety record the event has enjoyed over the years, in which the Zebras (Launch Directors) play a key role. Balloon Fiesta is one of few events of its kind, which allow spectator access to the launch field. This makes for a special close-up and personal experience, and one of the reasons why Balloon Fiesta has become the most photographed event on the planet. In any given year mass ascension can include 500 or more balloons, and with attendance averaging 80,000 people per day . . . this could be a recipe for "mass mayhem" if it weren't for the Zebras.

During a mass ascension, balloons are launched in waves of approximately 250, beginning with the downwind rows. Zebras are in communication with all pilots prior to and during the launch sequence via verbal and/or accepted visual signals. The Zebras let the pilots know where they will be standing, order of launch, and what hand signals to look for

during the launch sequence. They also discuss wind conditions and the balloon traffic directly overhead. Zebras clear each balloonist for take-off, and if required, they'll direct the pilot and crew to walk the balloon out to an unobstructed area next to their launch site. When the skyway is clear, the Zebra blows their whistle and gives a "thumbs up" signal letting the pilot know they are "good" to launch. Zebras are responsible for directing and controlling spectator crowds for all launches and special events such as balloon glows. They also advise pilots and safety officials on matters pertaining to equipment safety, including airworthiness and airmanship, checking to see there is no visual damage to either the envelope or gondola.

Dressed in striped black & white uniforms, much like football referees, Zebras wear their stripes proudly and take their jobs very seriously. The team of Zebras involves 70 plus people. New volunteers are referred to as ZITS (Zebras in Training). Everyone must go through intensive classroom and field training for two years before being allowed to direct their own launch sequences.

GOING ALOFT

Launching a hot air balloon is generally much easier than landing one. The expansive grass-covered launch field of Balloon Fiesta Park provides the ideal site, capable of accommodating an average of 250 balloons at a time. A mass ascension at Balloon Fiesta will encompass 500 or more balloons, which are launched from the park in waves. Once successfully aloft, the pilot's attention is focused on maintaining a safe clearance from other balloonists above, below and to the side. Pilots constantly assess wind speed and direction altering their altitude as necessary by ascending (firing the burners) or descending (releasing air from the envelope). Watchful eyes are required of pilot and passengers who continually look for any fixed obstacles that may lie in the flight path such as radio or transmission towers and lines, building structures and trees.

Flight duration is generally limited between one and two hours, depending on the quantity of propane gas, number of passengers on board, and the amount of maneuvering (burner firing) required. With ever-changing air temperature, wind speed and direction, selecting an appropriate landing site is an ongoing flight challenge. From the moment of launch, landing is on the pilots' minds. The site must have an unobstructed low fly-in approach, minimal ground obstacles such as fences, boulders, light poles or trees, and most importantly, "chase" vehicle access. Complicating the landing site selection further is the fact that Albuquerque is becoming more and more densely populated with less "open space" designations.
There are also "Prohibited Zones" (PZ's) and "Sensitive Areas" (SA's) within urban settings, which can also impact landing opportunities.
We'll discuss landings in more detail a little later.

THE RIO GRANDE SPLASH & DASH

Albuquerque offers balloonists a unique opportunity with access to the Rio Grande. If the winds are right, blowing from the launch field in a westerly direction, accomplished pilots have the potential to execute a "Splash & Dash". This challenging maneuver entails a low fly-in above the trees that border the river, at which point, the pilot initiates a rapid descent towards the water allowing the bottom of the gondola to skim the surface. To avoid landing in the water or on a sandbar, at just the right moment, the pilot must fire up the burner(s) in order to gain enough altitude to clear the tree tops on the ascent. The winds don't always cooperate to allow the execution of a "Splash & Dash". However, if you're one of those fortunate enough to be onboard when the pilot goes for a dip in the river, it makes for an exhilarating and memorable flight.

The Landing . . . What goes up must come down

FINDING A LANDING SITE

To quote one pilot "launching is optional but landing is mandatory". Another pilot commented that "all balloon landings are controlled crashes, because balloons have little navigational control. If you land and walk away from it, then it's considered a good landing!"

OFFICIAL COMPETITION MAP WITH PROHIBITED ZONES (PZ'S)

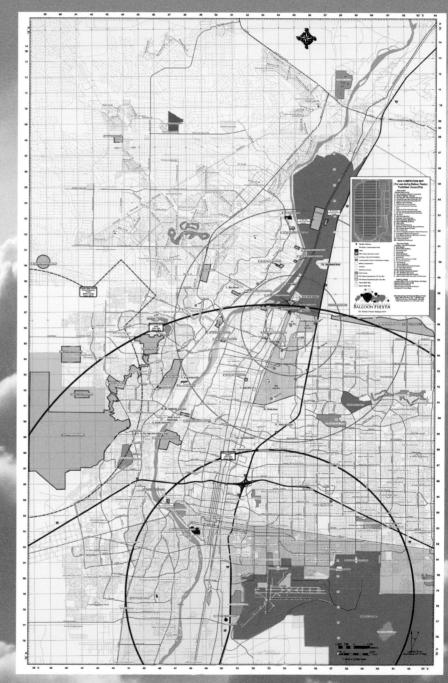

Considering the number of balloons that fly during Balloon Fiesta, it's gratifying to know, especially if you are a passenger, that few balloonists experience unsuccessful landings. At the onset of each year's event, all registered pilots are given an official aerial grid map of Albuquerque's Rio Grande Valley with current information on Prohibited Zones (PZs) and Sensitive Areas (SAs) as designated by AIBF. (Refer to the AIBF Aerial Naviagtion Map) Additionally, pilots must adhere to all Federal Aviation Regulations (FARs) set forth in the valley area.

Prohibited Zones (PZs) are areas where, in the interest of safety or landowner relations, balloons may not be launched or landed, and in some circumstances shall not fly over at less than a specified altitude. These are highlighted on the official map in YELLOW and RED with the location and hazard description denoted on the back of the map. A YELLOW PZ is a restricted area where no launches or landings are permitted. A RED PZ will also include a minimum allowable altitude. Only in an emergency are pilots allowed to land their balloons in a Prohibited Zone.

Sensitive Areas (SAs) are areas where pilots may land as long as they exercise extra caution and follow correct retrieval procedures. One may not launch from a Sensitive Area. These zones are designated on the official map in PURPLE, with location, hazard description, and special retrieval procedures on the back of the map.

54

The ideal landing area in the Rio Grande Valley is towards the west as there are far fewer Prohibited Zones and more open space. Flying and finding landing sites in an easterly direction from the launch field is difficult not only because of the Sandia Mountains but also because of the density of the populated residential areas. Native American pueblo lands lie to the north and northeast, the majority of which are designated as SAs. To the south lie downtown and the airport. For obvious reasons trying to land in this part of Albuquerque can challenge the most experienced balloonist.

A FUN, FUNNER, AND FUNNEST LANDING

Fun, funner, and funnest is how one pilot described possible landings on a commercial balloon flight. Needless to say the passengers were intrigued to learn more . . . or maybe not!

A "fun" landing is when the winds are calm and the pilot gently sets the basket on the ground in an up-right position. Everyone remains in the basket acting as ballast while the chase crew and/or bystanders help deflate the envelope. If there is no one around to assist, the pilot will try to keep the envelope inflated until the chase crew arrives. However, if ground winds are present causing the envelope to blow around the pilot might initiate its deflation on his own. This may be necessary in order to prevent the basket and those on-board being dragged across the ground.

One can experience a "funner" landing if the ground winds are variable or in excess of 10 mph, making the landing conditions not all that gentle. In some cases, this might cause the basket to hit and bounce along the ground several times before coming to rest... hopefully, in an up-right position but not always! Definitely, one does not leave the basket until the envelope is deflated or otherwise as directed by the pilot. A "funner" landing experience can also be enhanced by the type of terrain you end up bouncing across... needless to say a scrubby, rocky, cactus filled desert would be a less than desirable landing spot. However, sometimes there is just no choice and the pilot has to make a split second decision to "drop anchor".

The "funnest" landings (while not all that humorous for pilot and passengers) can entail a variety of situations and are the type one might end up seeing on the Ten O'clock News. Getting the envelope caught up on a radio tower, in a tree, or bouncing across rough terrain are all considered "funnest" landings.

BREAKING DOWN AND PACKING UP

Saving the best for last…now back safely on terra firma and in one piece, thinking the fun is over…wait, not so fast! With the help of the chase crew, who hopefully have successfully found the landing site, its time to pack it all up! Oh, by the way, if you're looking for a ride back to the launch site, participating in the breakdown and pack up should be considered a given. Keep your fingers crossed that the pilot landed in a location with chase vehicle access, otherwise "Popeye", hope you had spinach for breakfast, because you're going to need it! Depending on the size of the envelope, basket, and number of propane tanks, the combined weight of the balloon components can range anywhere between 500 to 700 pounds or more. Having to haul this equipment out over rough terrain is not a fun way to end a beautiful balloon flight.

Once the envelope has been deflated, it must be packed into a canvas bag for storage and transport. In order to do this, all the air must first be removed. Starting from the basket end several people will line-up to lift and gather the fabric of the envelope squeezing the air from it. They continue moving towards the crown (top) of the balloon, until all the air has been removed. Those taking part in this process are known as "squeezers".

Large envelopes are typically packed up, starting from the crown; 2-3 crew members will hold and walk a canvas storage bag towards the basket, as others continue stuffing the fabric into it. If you have a large number of crew, sometimes they will pick up and stuff the envelope into the storage bag, while it remains stationary. Occasionally, a couple of people will sit on the bag to remove any excess air. Once the envelope is packed, it will be placed in the chase vehicle. The burner system is removed and stored along with the disassembled basket frame. The basket itself is now ready to be mounted back onto the chase vehicle. In many cases chase vehicles will employ hydraulic lift gates used both for lifting and storing the basket, as they can be quite bulky and heavy to handle.

As previously discussed, balloon envelopes are generally not washed, primarily because they are difficult to get thoroughly dry, and washing removes special coatings. If mildew and mold forms on the fabric, it can weaken the material and seams thereby shortening the life of the envelope. Due to this fact, balloonists will often include an expansive nylon drop cloth as part of their accessories. If the ground is moist or dirty, it can be unfurled in order to keep the envelope dry and clean, at launch or during the pack up process.

Now its time to celebrate! Many times following a successful flight, there is a tradition to open and share a bottle of champagne among those who participated. A toast is made, quoting the "Balloonist's Prayer" (more about this tradition later) and the pilot is thanked for an experience of a lifetime!

Special Shape Balloons

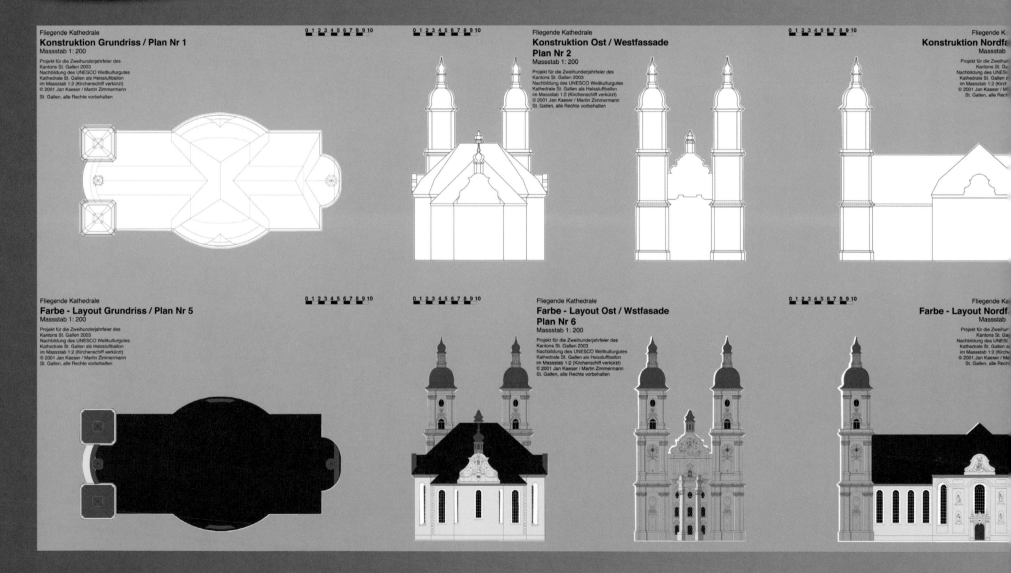

KUBICEK BALLOONS PROUDLY PRESENTS *ALOFT!* **SPECIAL SHAPE BALLOONS**

/ Plan Nr 3

utes
ion
rzt)
ann

/ Plan Nr 7

des
ion
allon
nn

Fliegende Kathedrale
Farbe - Layout Südfassade / Plan Nr 8
Massstab 1 : 200

Projekt für die Zweihundertjahrfeier des
Kantons St. Gallen 2003
Nachbildung des UNESCO Weltkulturgutes
Kathedrale St. Gallen als Heissluftballon
im Massstab 1:2 (Kirchenschiff verkürzt)
© 2001 Jan Kaeser / Martin Zimmermann
St. Gallen, alle Rechte vorbehalten

0 1 2 3 4 5 6 7 8 9 10

FABRICATING & FLYING SPECIAL SHAPES

Special shape hot air balloons are defined as enve-lopes having a non-standard elliptical or spherical shape. This would also include envelopes, which appear to have a standard shape (defined as "round" or "teardrop"), but with protruding appendages, such as eye balls, tails or ears. Standard shape hot air balloons have had a long history of using "printed images" on the envelope as a means of advertising promotion, but special shapes have taken that to a whole new level. Special shape envelopes began to emerge in the early 1970's as a more creative form of advertising, promoting everything from corporations to well-known products, characters, toys, and icons. Today, with available fabrics, sophisticated computer software and sew-ing equipment, creating a unique special shape envelope is limited only by one's imagination. Complicated designs can test the skills of the manufacturing team, as the end product must prove airworthy and meet FAA certification. The ultimate challenge though, falls on the pilot and crew that have to inflate, launch, land and deflate these special shape balloons.

Kubicek Balloons in the Czech Republic is a noted "special shape" balloon manufacturer and shares some of their insight into the design/development process. A customer will present a concept which includes some basic information, including photographs and even possibly a model. The icon used in this example is the St. Gallen Cathedral in Switzerland. As not every shape is ideal for a constructing (such as a needle shape) it is sometimes necessary to make some adaptations, for example, in proportions. While almost anything can be envisioned as an envelope form, at the end of the day, the design must be an airworthy aircraft. So the engineering team needs to factor in weight, safety, flying qualities and of course, the cost.

As an initial step in the process, a three dimensional graphic design of the special shape is created. The envelope drawings along with the specified equipment such as basket, burner system, propane tanks and accessories are presented to the customer. Once the design and cost are approved, a completion date is set, and a contract is signed. The meticulous effort of the designers now begins. This will entail hundreds of hours of work to create detailed three-dimensional design drawings using a specially developed software design system. A sophisticated system of ropes, straps and fabric ribs inside the envelope are used to maintain its shape, all which must be defined in the drawings. This construction technique allows a special shape balloon to become an aircraft and an aircraft to become a special shape balloon. Throughout the design process, the engineers will be calculating the strength of all the components that make up the balloon. All these calculations will later be checked by the Civil Aviation Authority.

Now the activity moves from the technicians to the seamsters and painters. Kilometers of fabric, (cut into thousands of 2-D panels by the special CNC cutter) tapes and lines have to all be sewn together in accordance with the drawing and design specifications. The moment of the truth comes during the first inflation. The designers and seamsters nervously wait, hoping that something doesn't go wrong causing them to undo, fix and re-sew a section of the envelope. Any small adjustments and final finishing touches are made and the balloon is then ready for its maiden flight. During this inflation and launch process a specific set of tasks are carried out to confirm the flying qualities of the balloon. How much to climb, how much to descend, how to maneuver, how to lift, how to land.

Depending on the size and complexity of the design, special shape balloons, if they are rotation shape (cans or bottles) can cost 2-3 times more than a standard shape. Non-rotational special shape (cubes or mascots) can cost 3-4 times that of standard shape balloons. Price can further be impacted by the amount of artwork required to replicate the original image. The St. Gallen Cathedral balloon was one of the more complicated designs and entailed a lot of artwork, making it one of the most expensive that Kubicek Balloons has produced.

Special shape balloons take considerably more effort to inflate and fly than do standard shape balloons. From prep to launch, to land and pack up,more time and crew are required. Typically, the envelopes are much larger making them quite bulky and heavy, and more difficult to unpack and pack up. Obviously wind is not a friend of the special shape balloon. Even during the cold inflate, which can exceed 40 minutes, the crew can been seen holding down multiple crown lines to keep the envelope stable. After heating the envelope and getting the balloon up righted, many times it will remain tethered on the ground rather than launch in anything but light wind conditions.

SPECIAL SHAPE RODEO™

At the 1989 Balloon Fiesta, 28 special shape balloons inflated and launched from Balloon Fiesta Park one afternoon. The event resulted in a large crowd gathering on the launch field. It also caused a traffic jam on the adjoining roadways as drivers slowed to watch the awe inspiring balloons float across the Rio Grande Valley. The theme oriented mass ascension proved to be so popular that event organizers added it to the regular program schedule, and named it the "Special Shape Rodeo".

Special shape participation at Balloon Fiesta continued to grow year after year, reaching a peak in 1996 when 108 balloons took part in the Rodeo. Considering the extended inflation time of these balloons, and the ideal weather conditions required for launching and flying them, to witness a mass ascension of special shapes is quite spectacular. Balloon Fiesta currently dedicates two mornings of their nine day event for inflating and launching of special shape balloons. It is such a crowd pleaser, that many ballooning events worldwide now include a special shape activity as part of their regular program.

70

Airabelle #3
Born: 2004
Size: 220,000 cu ft
Weight: 950 lbs
Owner: Dean Foods
FAA Registration: N8282
Home Town: Albuquerque, NM

Joey Bee (blue shoes and nose)
Born: September 2003
Size: 98,000 cu. ft.
Weight: 480 lbs.
Owners: Aerial Marketing, LLC
FAA Registration: 997LB
Home Town: Peoria, AZ

Joelly Baby Bee (purple shoes and nose)
Born: August 2010
Size: 56,000 cu. ft.
Weight: 200 lbs.
Owners: Aerial Marketing, LLC
FAA Registration: 995LB
Home Town: Peoria, AZ

Lilly Bee (red shoes and nose)
Born: September 2003
Size: 98,000 cu. ft.
Weight: 480 lbs.
Owners: Aerial Marketing, LLC
FAA Registration: 998LB
Home Town: Peoria, AZ

America's Challenge™ Gas Balloon Race

BACKGROUND AND OVERVIEW

The first organized attempt to turn ballooning into a "spectator sport" can be accredited to the 19th century James Gordon Bennett, Jr., a newspaper millionaire. Both a sportsman and sports promoter, he conceived a series of international long distance balloon races on September 30, 1906. The inaugural race was titled the Coupe Aeronautique Gordon Bennett. Propane fueled hot air balloons had yet to be invented, so gas balloons were the aircraft of the day. Success at the time was measured in either distance or duration. For the Gordon Bennett series, the winner was considered to be the pilot who flew the farthest distance, measured from the launching point. One key factor in winning a gas balloon race is that pilots must land on terra firma. If they have the misfortune of landing in the water, it is grounds for disqualification.

The America's Challenge Gas Balloon Race was founded by the Albuquerque International Balloon Fiesta (AIBF) in 1995. This vision was largely due to the efforts of Mark Sullivan, a former Balloon Fiesta President and recipient of two Montgolfier Diplomes (one of the Sport's highest honors). A renowned competitor in all the major gas ballooning events, Sullivan believed that the United States should have its own premier gas ballooning event. Modeled on the Coupe Aeronautique Gordon Bennett Race, America's Challenge differs from the original event by allowing balloons from all countries, without a limit on the number of entries from each. The inaugural America's Challenge Race broke distance records dating all the way back to 1912. Balloon Fiesta has hosted the Coupe Aeronautique Gordon Bennett several times. The country hosting the event is determined by the winning balloonist from the previous year.

Gas balloons sustain flight as a result of lifting gas pumped into their envelopes. Helium and hydrogen are typically used, both of which are lighter than air. However, hydrogen while less expensive, costing approximately $1,500 per inflation, is highly volatile (remember the Hindenburg?) and special care is required during the fill process. Inflating the envelope with helium, on the other hand, can cost in excess of $6,000 for two to three days of flight time. Gas balloons generally launch just after dusk, when the winds are most calm. The initial preparation of the envelope and outfitting the basket takes several hours, and can start as early as midday. To inflate a gas balloon, a fuel hose from a compressed gas tanker truck is inserted into the "neck" or bottom of the envelope. These types of balloons maintain a much smaller diameter opening than do hot air balloons. The inflation process of multiple balloons can take several hours to complete. Once each balloon is filled the hose is removed and the envelope is sealed.

Gas balloon pilots basically have two ways to control their altitude. To descend, they can either vent gas through the crown of the envelope or wait for the cooler evening temperatures to contract the gas in the envelope. To ascend pilots have two options. They can drop or reduce ballast, which is suspended by ropes on the outside of the basket. Ballast containers are typically comprised of sand, rather than water, which can freeze in cold weather and high altitude. The second option is to wait for warmer daytime temperatures to heat the gas causing the envelope to expand, which creates lift. Gas balloonists prefer surface winds to be below twelve miles per hour for launching and landing. The distance and duration they travel, will greatly depend on the upper atmospheric winds and prevailing weather conditions. Sometimes the weather can be cold, dangerous and violent, testing both the skills and stamina of pilots. There have been many cases where gas balloon races were delayed or canceled all together, simply because the existing and forecasted weather conditions were too unpredictable, putting lives at risk.

Gas balloon races launching from Albuquerque have achieved impressive flight distances over the years, in some cases reaching the East Coast of the US and Canada. Six separate competitions resulted in four completed flight distances of greater than 1,200 miles (2,000 km); and 12 completed flights in competitions have resulted in distances of more than 900 miles (1,500 km). One of the longest distance records achieved at AIBF was set by the team of Davies & Davis aloft for more than 60 hours. They traveled across 1,448.49 miles (2,331.17 km) at the inaugural 1995 event. However, this team received mileage penalties due to official protests from other competitors, and ultimately the distance record was awarded to the winning team of Abruzzo & Melton, who flew 1,392.90 miles (2,241.71 km).

NIGHT MAGIC GLOW™, SPECIAL SHAPE GLOWDEO™ AND TWILIGHT TWINKLE GLOW™

Balloon Fiesta offers many special events for attendees to enjoy over the course of nine days. However, one of the biggest crowd pleasers is the various "balloon glows" occuring throughout the week. Balloon Fiesta has trademarked many of these events with specific names such as Twilight Twinkle Glow, Special Shape Glowdeo and Night Magic Glow. While their names may vary, all the balloon glows entail the assembly of inflated and tethered balloons on the launch field, weather permitting of course. As the evening sky grows dark, the command is given for pilots to ignite their burners. The volume of glowing envelopes forms a variety of patterns and designs appearing like giant Christmas ornaments and burning candles. These popular evening glows draw many "oohs" and "aahs" from the gathered crowds, making it one of the highlights of Balloon Fiesta.

86

It is believed the concept of nighttime balloon glows was started when 19 balloonists gathered for a 1979 Christmas Eve celebration at the Albuquerque Country Club. Thereafter word of the nighttime glows spread. Scott Appelman, an AIBF board member at the time, had attended such events in Longview, TX and Durango, CO and decided to pitch the idea to his fellow board members. At its event in 1987 Balloon Fiesta launched the world's largest balloon glow with over 225 participants and an estimated 100,000 people in attendance. Today breathtaking "glows" are held at ballooning events world over.

FLIGHT OF THE NATIONS

Registration of balloons and pilots at Balloon Fiesta each year always includes numerous entries from outside the United States. The number of foreign participants varies from year to year depending on both schedules and funding resources. Shipping both envelope and basket into Albuquerque from overseas by air can prove to be very expensive. At the 2008 event, there were an incredible number of foreign balloonists registered from 22 different countries.

The purpose of the Flight of the Nations is to honor all countries participating in the Albuquerque International Balloon Fiesta. It involves the midweek mass ascension with a maximum of two balloons from each registered nation. Balloons are launched by country in succession, with their nation's flag proudly displayed on the crown line or basket while their respective national anthems are played over the launch field public address system. The Flight of the Nations occurs just after the "sponsor of the day" balloon launches, with the regular mass ascension following.

FLYING COMPETITIONS

Each year Balloon Fiesta holds series of flying competitions, that take place during the week. Pilots earn points in daily competitions with high scores resulting in high overall rankings. In addition their accumulated points establish the overall championship winners. The winning stakes can be worth the effort. In a recent year the first place champion took home $10,000. The participating pilots are assigned a series of bar-coded markers that they use in each competition for scoring. After launching, they are not permitted to receive assistance from other people, nor touch the ground, until their markers are thrown, and they have cleared the target area. However, pilots are permitted to make multiple passes over a given target area, as long as the maneuvers are completed within the set time constraints of the competition. The following provides a brief description of the various flying competitions, where flying finesse and accuracy play key roles.

Multiple Judge Declared Goal (MJDG) competitions are events with pilots launching from Balloon Fiesta Park and flying to any one of the designated off-field targets. The intent is to drop a "marker" as close as possible to the center of the designated target.

Fly-In-Task (FIT) competitions are events where pilots launch from a site of their own choice, excluding Prohibited Zones (PZs) and Sensitive Areas (SAs) and no closer than one statute mile from the center of the launch field. They will fly in to the target area(s) at Balloon Fiesta Park where they will attempt to drop a "marker" on the designated target.

Balloon Fiesta Hold'em competitions take place on the cleared Balloon Fiesta Park launch field. Each participant will be given five (5) "common cards" which includes the Ace, King, Queen of Hearts, as well as the 8 and 9 of Clubs. The objective is for the pilot to build the best poker hand by flying in and over the field dropping two markers on any of the 15 different displayed "target" cards, trying to achieve the best score possible. The scoring results from Hold'em do not count as part of the pilots overall competition scores.

Pole Grab (also known as the "Key Grab," as the grand prize may include the keys to a new truck or car) competitions are events where pilots launch from a site of their choice, excluding PZs and SAs, and no closer than one statute mile from the center of the launch field. The object is to fly in to the target area at Balloon Fiesta Park and retrieve one of the envelopes attached to the top of each pole that are approximately 30 ft. high. There will be up to five (5) poles in the target area. Capturing any one of the envelopes will earn the pilot a prize. However, only one random envelope will contain the grand prize. If wind conditions permit, pilots may make multiple attempts to retrieve an envelope, but only one envelope is allowed per pass. Retrieval attempts may not involve the use of any tool or capture device, and are limited to the hands of any person in the gondola whose feet must remain planted on the floor.

95

Balloon Fiesta Golf competitions, if conducted, involve the use of the golf greens at the south end of the launch field at Balloon Fiesta Park. The object of the competition is for the pilot to drop his/her marker on the outlined golf green closest to the pin (flag). Markers that land within the outlined golf greens will score. Each marker will be measured from the weighted portion to that green's pin. Shortest distance is best.

Balloon Fiesta Drop and Double Drop competitions, if conducted, involve competitors dropping their markers in designated scoring areas as close as possible to the target. For the Balloon Fiesta Drop, the scoring area is defined by a circle around an "X" with a 200' radius. The one closest to the center wins. For the Double Drop, the scoring area is defined as two opposite "V's". The pilot must drop one marker inside each "V", the one with placement closest to the intersection wins.

Special Shape Rodeo participants earn points when flying their special shape balloons. All special shape balloons launching from Balloon Fiesta Park must be inflated and launched (weather permitting) by the times designated by the Balloonmeister at those particular briefings. With appropriate permission pilots are allowed to fly special shape balloons in the other competitions. Competition for this event takes into consideration the challenges of flying special shape balloons and can include a Multiple Judge Declared Goal, Pole Grab or Balloon Fiesta Drop.

COLLECTIBLES

With the Albuquerque International Balloon Fiesta (AIBF) having a forty year history behind it, there are great opportunities for both seasoned and would-be collectors. Each year Balloon Fiesta authorizes the creation of an original poster and an array of official pins and patches, among other memorabilia. In addition many of the pilots, especially those flying special shape balloons, offer up collectible pins of their iconic balloons. Some pilots produce multiple pin designs, some used for trading and others used as flight mementos. Balloon trading cards have also become popular with collectors, providing a more affordable way of trading and collecting. Of all the AIBF collectibles, pins are still the most desired and traded. In addition to individual balloon pins, one can find a variety of other types of pins including those from sponsors like UPS or Pepsi. There are also pins dedicated to specific events or subjects such as Dawn Patrol or the Zebras. Even some of the AIBF Board Members create personalized pins each year.

How much are some of the AIBF collectibles worth? It boils down to supply and demand. How many are out there, how popular is it, who wants it and how much are they willing to pay for it? Some Balloon Fiesta pins that originally cost a few dollars twenty years ago might be fetching $50 or more today. Rare and unusual pins produced in limited quantities may bring $300 or more, again based upon supply and demand.

It is easy to spot both long time balloon goers as well as those into serious collecting. Each may be wearing clothing, including hats of a historical Balloon Fiesta nature, adorned with highly collectible pins, patches or other items of note. Steve Stucker, the KOB-TV (local NBC station) weatherman is a prime example, having attended Balloon Fiesta for nearly a quarter of a century. He shows up to the event each year wearing an iconic pin filled ¾ length white coat and a balloon shaped hat both displaying his passion and history of collecting.

Ty Young, an AIBF Board Member, is one who also knows and has written about collecting Balloon Fiesta memorabilia. He provided rare access to a warehouse full of his Balloon Fiesta collectibles that he has been hoarding away for years. While he may not admit to it, Ty is clearly a full-blown addict when it comes to collecting, and it goes way beyond AIBF memorabilia. However, he must realize he can't trust himself as there is a sign hanging in his office that reads, "DON'T BUY ANYTHING!"

THE ANDERSON-ABRUZZO ALBUQUERQUE INTERNATIONAL BALLOON MUSEUM

A trip to Balloon Fiesta would not be complete without a visit to the Anderson-Abruzzo Albuquerque International Balloon Museum. The museum which operates independently from Balloon Fiesta, opened in 2005 is located on the southern edge of Balloon Fiesta Park. It features an array of world-class ballooning exhibits, equipment and memorabilia covering the history of the sport. Collections include items donated by renowned balloonists, as well as by ballooning and history enthusiasts from around the world. The museum was also fortunate enough to receive the Soukup and Thomas International Balloon and Airship Museum collection, donated to the City of Albuquerque through the City of Mitchell, South Dakota in 2000.

The museum was named in honor of two Albuquerque pilots who were pioneers in long-distance gas balloon flight. Ben Abruzzo and Maxie Anderson were part of the crews who in 1978 were the first to successfully cross the Atlantic in a balloon. Not to leave a stone unturned, the team made a successful crossing of the Pacific Ocean in 1981. The museum showcases the spirit of adventure of these and many other balloonists from around the world.

AFTERGLOW™ FIREWORKS SHOW

While launch activities consume balloon goers in the early morning hours, thousands of people are drawn back to Balloon Fiesta Park for an array of nighttime festivities, including the glows, great music, and good eating. However, one of the biggest evening attractions is the spectacular AfterGlow Fireworks Show which takes place five out of nine nights (weather permitting).

Starfire Pyrotechnics has been producing the fireworks show at Balloon Fiesta since 1985. It all started when Board Member, Charlie Hines wanted to celebrate his wife's birthday, which coincided with the event. Charlie opened his wallet and asked Starfire owners Anita Cates and John Cates what $300 would buy him in the way of fireworks in honor of his wife's birthday. Subsequently, a tradition began of shooting a small fireworks display before the weekend morning pilot briefings. Over the years, fireworks at Balloon Fiesta evolved into mesmerizing light shows with over a ton of pyrotechnics being ignited each of the five nights to the delight of the crowd.

The fireworks show does not come cheaply . . . The average cost per minute is $1,000 for the aerial displays and $3,000 for the "candle line" which stretches 1,200 feet on the west side of the launch field.

NOMENCLATURE AND COST

Your ballooning journey would not be complete without knowing some basic technical information about hot air balloons . . . how they work, how they're made, and how much they cost. We hope this knowledge will enhance your overall appreciation for the sport of ballooning and for all the pilots who fly them.

A hot air balloon is comprised of three main components: the envelope (fabric which contains the hot air); the propane/burner system (used for heating the air); and basket (or gondola) which serves as the pilot/passenger and propane storage compartment. The following diagrams highlight the basic equipment components referred to throughout this section.

THROAT (mouth)

SCOOP (half) SKIRT (full)

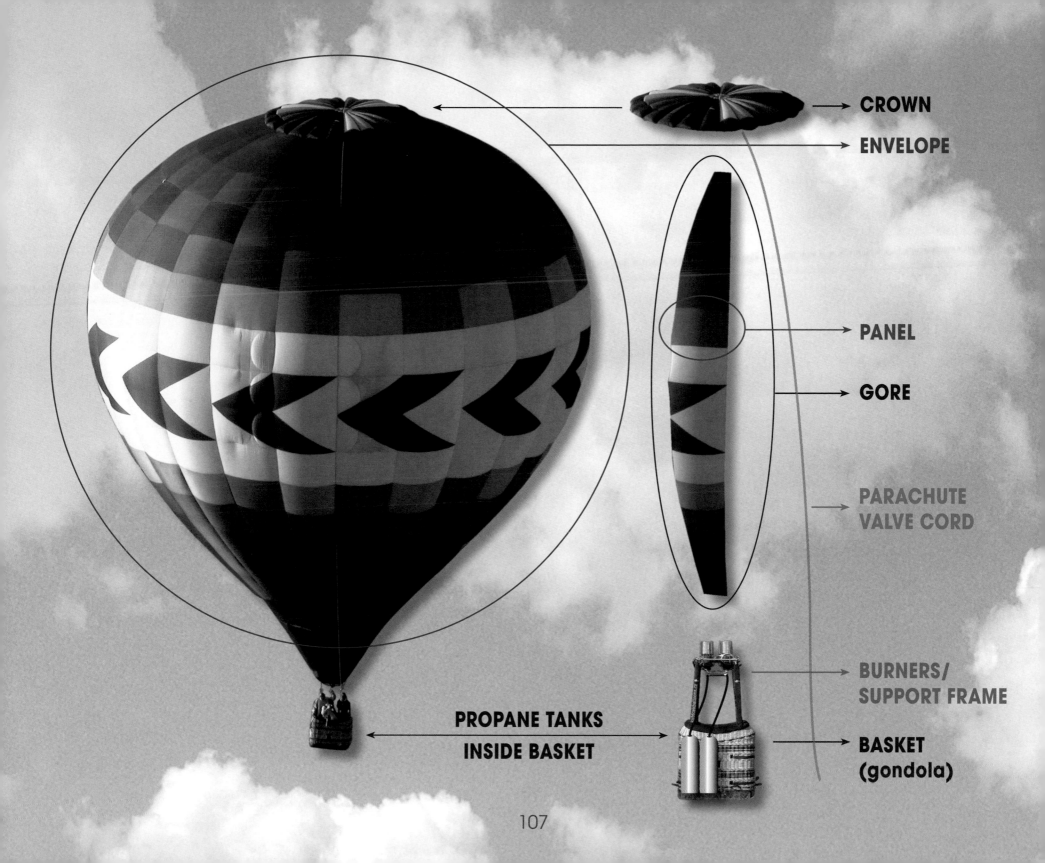

CROWN

ENVELOPE

PANEL

GORE

PARACHUTE
VALVE CORD

BURNERS/
SUPPORT FRAME

PROPANE TANKS
INSIDE BASKET

BASKET
(gondola)

HOW DO THEY WORK?

The basic principle of lift involves the heating of warm air using a burner/propane system and the air is then captured inside the balloon envelope. The balloon rises because the warm air is lighter than the cooler air it replaces. The size (mass) of the envelope is typically defined in a measurement of cubic feet (meters). In order to lift "x" number of pounds off the ground (combined weight of the envelope, burner/propane system, basket and passengers), "y" number cubic feet of heated air (size or mass of the envelope) is required. The size of the envelope determines the load or carrying capacity. The smallest one-person, basketless balloons, called "Cloudhoppers", entail an envelope mass in the range of 21,000 cubic feet. At the opposite end of the scale are the commercial balloons used for group flights or sightseeing tours that can carry 24 or more people. The envelopes used for this purpose can entail a mass of up to 600,000 cubic feet. Generally speaking, the typical balloon envelope is in the range of 100,000 cubic feet, and can carry 3-5 people. The empty weight for these types of balloons, with two filled propane tanks will average approximately 600 pounds.

Once aloft, the means of piloting a hot air balloon are very basic. In order to ascend or increase altitude, the gas valve is activated, and the burner(s) fired, sending warm air into the envelope, creating lift. The longer the gas valve is opened, the more heat is generated and the faster the balloon will rise. Heated air will not escape from the throat (mouth) of the envelope because heat rises and keeps moving in an upward direction. To descend or reduce altitude, the pilot activates a "parachute valve" (not to be confused with the propane or gas valve) located at the crown (top) of the envelope. The valve is basically a large opening at the crown of the balloon covered with a self-sealing circle of fabric. The vent lines connect around the edge and converge in the center, (like the multiple lines on a parachute, hence the name). They are tied to a control cord that runs through the center of the envelope to the basket. Pulling on the cord opens the valve, thus releasing warm air out of the envelope to either slow ascent or cause descent. Many envelopes also have secondary openings known as rip panels or vents, used to rotate the balloon. This allows for reorienting the direction of the basket for landings. Upon landing, the parachute valve can be opened to release the air and collapse the envelope.

A change in altitude may also result in a change to the balloon's direction, which is impacted by wind. Wind patterns are affected by both weather and geographic conditions. The "Box Effect" of the Rio Grande Valley discussed in an earlier section explains in greater detail how wind patterns change at different altitudes.

HOW ARE THEY MADE?

Hot air balloon envelope shapes are generally defined by four design categories: the most typical design and the one most seen during Balloon Fiesta, is the round sphere (or bulb shape) balloon; the football, a more aerodynamic shape, is used for racing and competition events; the more atypical tetrahedron shape is described as an upside down triangle shape; and lastly are special shape balloons that include bulb shapes with appendages as well as irregular non-conforming shapes.

Envelope fabric is woven from one of two types of material, rip-stop nylon or Dacron (polyester). Some manufacturers prefer the lighter nylon fabric while others use Dacron, which is heavier. There are advantages and disadvantages to both. Nylon is a lighter and stronger material, but Dacron can withstand higher temperatures. Load tapes and cords are elements sewn into the gore panels that help maintain the envelope's shape and structural integrity. Gore panels are the sectional panels which extend from the throat (or mouth) to the crown and define the shape of the envelope. Gore panels are made up of smaller panels of fabric.

The nylon and Dacron fabrics are actually woven mesh structures that allow air to pass through them. In order to contain the heated air, the envelope fabric must be coated with a sealant. The most common sealant is a polyure-

thane coating. This coating also contains additives such as neoprene (synthetic rubber) or silicone, and an ultraviolet inhibitor to protect it from breaking down when exposed to sunlight. The mouth of the envelope is coated with a special fire-resistant material to prevent the propane burner from igniting it. The life expectancy of an envelope is approximately 400 flying hours.

Hot air balloons obtain their lift from burner systems using pressurized liquid propane, which is stored on-board the basket in light-weight aluminum, stainless steel or titanium cylinders, each containing 10-25 gallons. The typical 3-5 passenger balloon will carry two propane cylinders, which can each weigh 135 pounds or more when full. Average fuel consumption for this type of balloon is approximately 15-20 gallons an hour. A typical flight will last one to two hours. However, air temperature, weight, weather and of course the pilot, are all factors that can impact the duration. The burner unit is supported by a frame over the basket. The unit may further employ a gimbal system enabling the pilot to alter the flame direction in order to avoid overheating the envelope fabric. A burner may have a secondary propane valve to release propane to the burner without preheating it. This is referred to as a "whisper burner" and is generally used for flight over livestock or residential areas. It also generates a softer yellow flame, ideal for night glows.

A burner can be configured in a single, double, triple, and in some cases a quad set-up, depending on the mass of the envelope and lifting ratios. Burners vary in their thermal output ranging from approximately 15 to 50 million BTU's. The number of burners required will depend on the size of the envelope and overall weight. However, for the typical 3-5 person balloon, the average BTU output will be in the range of 15-30 million BTU's. The propane rapidly flows in a liquid form through hoses to the heating coil. The heating coil is a length of tubing arranged around the burner. When the pilot opens the valve, the propane flows in a liquid form and is ultimately ignited by a pilot light. As the flame burns, it heats up the metal tubing changing the propane from liquid to gas before it is ignited. This transition results in a "hotter" flame and more efficient fuel consumption.

Balloon baskets (gondolas), encompass the pilot/passenger compartment and have remained essentially unchanged since the 1700's. Wicker has been the long standing choice for the construction of baskets as this material is sturdy, flexible, and relatively lightweight. Because of its energy absorbing qualities, wicker reduces the impact force of landings for those onboard. In recent years, other materials have been explored for construction including fiberglass and aluminum. However, both were prone to collapsing upon a "funner" or "funnest" landing, as previously defined in the Landing section. While most basket designs

tend to be square or rectangular-shaped, later innovations included a triangular-shaped basket. This design configuration allows for some creative placement of the propane tanks and instrument panel.

Wicker baskets are typically made from rattan and willow, woven together. The top or edge of the basket sides is commonly bound In a torm of leather, providing some sott absorption to the compartment as well as protection to the basket itself when entering and exiting. The basket is typically connected to the burner unit and envelope through the use of stainless steel or Kevlar cables and/or upright rigid supports. The general life expectancy of a basket, assuming few "funnest" landings, is approximately 800 flying hours.

Hot air balloons do not have any true navigational controls like fixed-wing aircraft. However, pilots typically equip their balloons with a series of instruments, which assist in flying the craft. These include: an altimeter, a variometer, to track rate of climb (vertical speed), temperature gauges for both envelope air and ambient air readings, and a GPS system Io indicate ground speed and direction. Most pilots also carry 2-way radio communications on-board. This is important not only for communicating with the chase crew but also aviation authorities, should the balloon fliy into restricted areas.

HOW MUCH DO THEY COST?

The following will provide a range of costs for a typical balloon setup. However, keep in mind that prices can dramatically change once you start adding all the "bells and whistles". The cost of a good used balloon will average $15,000 to $25,000. For a new sport balloon expect to pay approximately $40,000. If you were to up-grade to a larger more elaborate balloon setup the range in cost can be from $55,000 to $80,000. Special shape balloons, if they are rotation shape (cans or bottles) can cost 2-3 times more than standard shapes. Non-rotational special shapes (cubes or mascots) can cost 3-4 times that of a standard shapes balloon.

There are also ancillary costs that need to be considered in pursuing this sport:

Flight training for a private pilot's certificate ($2,800-$5,000)
Balloon insurance ($700-$1,200/year)
Chase vehicle (pick-up truck, trailer or van)
Inflation fan ($900-$1,500)
Fuel ($30-$40/flying hour)
2-Way radios
Champagne (for those post-flight celebrations!)

PILOT REQUIREMENTS

Hot air ballooning can be an airborne addiction for those who like to watch and those who like to fly. The romance of the sport attracts new pilots every single year. Just as for pilots flying fixed-wing aircraft, balloonists must be certified by the Federal Aviation Administration (FAA). This certification encompasses two levels, a private rating and a commercial rating. The private pilot rating entails a minimum of 10 hours of flight time in an un-tethered balloon, six flights of which must include instructor supervision. Before a private pilot certificate can be issued, the individual must complete and pass a written exam, an oral exam, and have a flight check from an FAA official. The Knowledge Exam covers FAA regulations, meteorology and general ballooning rules. The minimum age for licensing is 16.

The requirements for a commercial rating are a bit more intense. The pilot applying for this rating must have a minimum of 35 hours of flight time under their belt. Twenty of the hours must be completed in a balloon while the other 15 can include time in other fixed-wing aircraft. Just as with a private certificate, the pilot must complete and pass a computerized Knowledge Exam and oral exam as well as have the specified flight check. Once the commercial certificate is in-hand, the pilot may operate and/or fly for ballooning operations "for hire". The commercial rating also allows the pilot to conduct flight instruction for novice balloonists. Some commercial pilots do earn their living at the sport by flying passengers for sightseeing adventures and/or flying corporate advertising balloons.

Pilots are required to renew their rating every two years by passing a flight review administered by a commercial balloon pilot. Furthermore, per FAA regulations, balloonists must meet air-traffic control requirements if they are flying in and around a controlled airport, requiring radio contact capability with controllers.

THE BEGINNING OF A TRADITION, OR SO LEGEND HAS IT. . .

In 1783, the first manned balloon flight occurred in Paris, France. At that time not much took to the air other than birds, or Fall leaves caught by the autumn wind. So one can only imagine the fright of the local farmers fixing their gaze upon a huge fire-breathing object falling from the sky and landing in their field. As the farmers raced towards this strange contraption with pitchforks, ready to attack and destroy it, the pilots Pilatre and Francois, offered them a bottle of champagne as a warm gesture of gratitude for allowing them to land safely in their field.

The tradition lives on today, in memory of that first courageous flight, with champagne (or sparkling wine) often being used in conjunction with a "Toast" upon many commercial hot air balloon landings.

THE "TOAST". . .

Authorship of the Balloonist's Prayer is unknown, but is believed to have been adapted from an old Irish sailor's prayer. Among many commercial balloonists it is recited as the champagne "Toast".

The Balloonist's Prayer

The winds have welcomed you with softness.
The sun has blessed you with its warm hands.
You have flown so high and so well
that God joined you in laughter
And set you gently back into
the loving arms of Mother Earth

Credits & Acknowledgements

PHOTO CREDITS

All photographs in this book were taken by Douglas Heller or Bobbi Valentine with the exception of the following:

Photos provided by AIBF

Page 15: Sid Cutter
Page 41: Dawn Patrol
Page 68: "Miss Daisy"
Page 72: "Matrioshka"
Page 73: "Felix the Cat"
Page 74: "Airabelle"
Page 76: "Pandy"
Page 77: "Koshari Gallup", "Hopper T Frog"
Page 90: "Continental Airlines"
Page 96: Marker Drop
Page 113: Triangular Basket
Page 116: Champagne Bottle Balloon

Photos by AIBF photographers:

Marvin Coon

Page 13: First Balloon Rally

Marla Geltner

Page 72: "Buddy"

David Villegas

Page 39: Above the Rio Grande
Page 81: Gas Balloons
Page 85: Gas Balloon Basket
Page 86: Twilight Twinkle Glow
Pages 87, 88, 89: Special Shape Glowdeo
Page 94: Pole Grab
Page 95: Key Grab

Photos by Frances Ehrenberg-Hyman

Page 76: "Puddle Jumper"
Page 118: New Mexico Sky

Photo by Kathy Boyle

Page 117: New Mexico Sunset

Photos by Greg Meland (www.gregmeland.com)

Page 32: Special Shape Rodeo
Page 67: "St. Gallen" Special Shape Balloon
Page 68: "Humpty Dumpty", "Energizer Hot Hare"
Page 69: "Patriot", "Nelly-B", "La Ristra"

Photo by Ty Young

Photos provided by Kubicek Balloons

THANK YOU

Paul Smith (AIBF Executive Director)
Gary Dewey (AIBF Merchandise Manager)
Ty Young (AIBF Board Member)
Thomas McConnell (AIBF Board Member)
Kathie Leyendecker (AIBF Media Relations)
Kristi Conley (AIBF Media Flight Coordinator)
Tom Condit (original book design concept)
Ethel Hess (Publisher, *New Mexico Magazine*)
Michael Olivera (website design)
Bette Brodsky (Special Projects Design Director,
   New Mexico Magazine)

Jeffrey Kravitz, Esq (Fox Rothschild LLP)
Richard White (IT services, RKW Enterprises)
Steve Stucker (KOB-TV)
Toni Bennett (ExtraSpace Storage)
Anita Cates and John Cates (Starfire Pyrotechnics)
David Stone (La Posada de Santa Fe)
Susan and Lee Berk
Betsy Ehrenberg
Kyla and Roger Thompson
Sabrina LeChat
New Mexico Glass Alliance
New Mexico Magazine
Santa Fe Friends of Jazz
Zia Film Distribution LLC

Balloon pilots for our media flights during Balloon Fiesta

Cliff Keller "TOVA"
David Bobel "THAT-A-WAY"
Michel Auzat "PIKO"
Douglas Gantt "HAM-LET"
Dave Reineke "SUNSATIONAL"
Cliff Keller "LILY"
Ken Tadolini "OUTLAW"

Special thanks to family, friends and colleagues who perused the text for typos and corrections, especially Frances Ehrenberg-Hyman, Eileen Hutchinson. Mary Olivera and Paul Smith.

KUBICEK BALLOONS
Brno, Czech Republic, EU
Tel.: +420 545 422 620
e-mail: info@kubicekballoons.eu
www.kubicekballoons.eu

ExtraSpace Storage
locations nationwide
(877) 710-0232
www.extraspace.com

New Mexico Magazine
495 Old Santa Fe Trail
Santa Fe, NM 87501
505-827-7447
www.nmmagazine.com

Zia Film Distribution LLC
369 Montezuma Ave. #320
Santa Fe, NM 87501
(505) 438-9299
www.ziavideo.com